Cooking on Purpose

Life Lessons Learned From the Kitchen

Life Lessons Learned From the Kitchen

DIANA RILEY

COOKING ON PURPOSE
Published by Purposely Created Publishing Group™

Copyright © 2016 Diana Riley

ALL RIGHTS RESERVED.

No part of this book may be reproduced, distributed or transmitted in any form by any means, graphics, electronics, or mechanical, including photocopy, recording, taping, or by any information storage or retrieval system, without permission in writing from the publisher, except in the case of reprints in the context of reviews, quotes, or references.

Printed in the United States of America
ISBN (ebook): 978-1-942838-37-1
ISBN (paperback): 978-1-942838-36-4

Special discounts are available on bulk quantity purchases by book clubs, associations and special interest groups. For details email: sales@publishyourgift.com or call (888) 949-6228.

For information logon to:
www.PublishYourGift.com

Table of Contents

ACKNOWLEDGEMENTS ... IX

DEDICATION ... XI

INTRODUCTION ... 1

CHAPTER 1

DISCOVERING WHO I AM ... 3

Lillie's Red Beans ... 10
Seafood Stuffed Bell Peppers ... 12
Baked Redfish ... 4
Creole Smothered Okra with Shrimp ... 15

CHAPTER 2

LESSONS OUTSIDE OF MAMA'S KITCHEN ... 17

Baked Gouda Cheese Grits ... 24
Southern Fried Catfish ... 25
Seafood Sauce Picante ... 26
Mardi Gras King Cake ... 27

Chapter 3

Journey into the Real World of Cooking... 29

Spinach Quiche Lorraine ... 36
Brioche ... 37
Ratatouille ... 39
Chicken Marsala ... 40

Chapter 4

Uncovering My Hidden Passion for Cooking ... 43

Shrimp and Sausage Jambalaya ... 48
Pumpkin Pecan Cheesecake ... 50
Pickled Okra Salad & Shrimp ... 52
Hoppin' John ... 53

Chapter 5

Conflicting Life Lessons ... 55

Parmesan Risotto ... 62
Lemon Buerre Blanc Asparagus ... 64
Seared Scallops ... 65
Chocolate Mousse ... 67

Chapter 6
Embracing My Call to Cook ... 69

Venison Chili Beans ... 74
Soulful of Cheese and Macaroni ... 76
Not Your Mama's Meatloaf ... 78
White Chocolate Bread Pudding ... 80

Chapter 7
Defining My Purpose as a Chef ... 81

Linda's Eggplant Rice Dressing ... 88
Mama's Old Fashioned Potato Salad ... 89
Braised Short Ribs ... 90
Southern Okra Succotash ... 91

Chapter 8
What You Can Learn in the Kitchen ... 93

Garlic Braised Osso Bucco ... 100
Roast Thyme Chicken ... 102
Thyme Butter Sauce ... 103

About the Author ... 104

Acknowledgements

This book has been a long time coming. Some things, though not denied, have been delayed, this book being one of them. Though the vision tarried, I waited and it came to pass. In my waiting, I was blessed and fortunate to pursue my dreams and seek God like never before. Thank You, God, for fostering the desires in my heart and never forsaking me.

I would like to thank my wonderful husband, Barry Sr., for allowing me to chase my dreams while he holds the family down, spiritually and financially. He has kept me grounded and is a pivotal part of keeping me focused on my goals. I humorously say that, if he hadn't given me three babies, I probably would have completed this book by now; but I know that's not true. This is all part of God's plan and His purpose. I thank God for my husband and all the intricate details of our marriage that have afforded me the time, energy, and investment to write this book. I love you always.

To my children, Lakaza, E.J., Jalik, Barry Jr., Bryce, and Brook-Lynne, who seek all of mama's attention and care: without all of you, this book would not be complete. Thank you for loving me unconditionally. You are my story, you are my life, you are the reason behind every decision I make. I do my best to balance your needs and my purpose, and, one day, you will understand why.

To my sisters (Rebecca, Sonny, and Zakara) and brothers (Edward, Ernest, Keith, and Donitello): I love you. You have been supportive, even though it doesn't always seem like it. Y'all give me an incentive to do what I do, because I know y'all are watching. I hope the legacy continues. To my sisters and brothers-in-law, Freddie, Rosalyn, Brandon, Laura, Meredith, James I love you too.

Thank you to my church family, my Pastor, Bishop, and First Lady Ford: you have inspired and encouraged me to go after the things of God. I would also like to thank my close friends and associates who played a role in my journey, investing and believing in me and for buying my book.

I saved the best for last: without my mama and my grandma, I would not be here. I want to thank them for all they have given me, instilled in me, and for caring and praying for me. To my mama, Linda in heaven, I miss you and I know you would be proud of me, because you always were. I never wanted to disappoint you and I thank you for giving me room to make mistakes and learn from them with compassion. You taught me how to care for my babies, but you forgot to teach me how to keep the house clean with kids the way you did. To my grandma, Lillie Mae, you are my heart and gift from God. I thank you for showing me how to serve others, even strangers, and for showing me, without saying a word, how to love your enemies. Thank you for teaching me how to cook, especially the red beans. Thank you both for sharing and caring. I love you.

Dedication

I would also like to dedicate this book to my dad, Bruce. You loved me with all your heart and it showed. I will never forget going to my grandparents (who never wanted me to leave) and you never wanting me to be out of your sight. Rest in peace Dad, Grandma "Wink," and Grandpa "Bugaloo" and Candy—I miss you. I also appreciate my stepdad for supporting me as a little girl and now. You took me in at five-years-old and have been my dad to this day. Thank you for showing me how to garden—I'm not as good as you, but I'm learning.

Introduction

I am a Christian, a mother, and a wife. I am also a military veteran of the Louisiana Army National Guard with which I served nine years, including one tour of duty and a year in Iraq. As a young woman, I didn't have direction and guidance as to what profession I wanted to pursue. When I was little, I played dress up or pretended to be a teacher or wanted to be an artist, but later in life, things happened. There have been certain instances when I thought I had it all together, only to find out it wasn't meant to be. I have had challenges in discovering who I really am. It's not easy being transparent and talking about your issues; still, I soon discovered that it's not about me, but about who God wants me to be.

This book is about my journey to find my purpose. I will talk about work experiences that are not always related to cooking, but have been life-altering choices I had to make to pursue my goals. I believe that the best lessons are learned through experiences. I did not choose my passion—it chose me. In these chapters, I will talk about my decision to pursue culinary occupations based on my passion and purpose for life and how it led me to be self-employed while being a wife and a mother. I will also define and express what the term "culinary arts" means, as well as discuss what its distinct purpose is in God's calling on my life.

At the end of the book, I will summarize the lessons I've learned on my journey to becoming a chef, offering my A's to your Q's. There are virtues that I learned in the kitchen: patience, consistency, determination, resilience, endurance, trust, discipline, and strength. These are characteristics that can carry you along in life on your journey to fulfill your purpose.

CHAPTER 1

Discovering Who I Am

"By the grace God has given me, I laid a foundation as a wise builder, and someone else is building on it. But each one should build with care."

1 Corinthians 3:10

I come from a family of good cooks and people who love to eat, our lives and family gatherings always being centered around food. When I was growing up, I was surrounded by people who taught me the secrets of cooking, especially my mama and grandmother. It all started when I was a little girl, about eight-years-old.

In Thibodaux, Louisiana, I grew up with my stay-at-home mom and my stepdad. I was the only child for a few years until my mama decided to become guardian to my cousin who was a year older than me. She raised us as sisters. We had a garden that my stepdad started and my mama and I were the caretakers of. Most of the vegetables we ate came from the garden. We would all pitch in harvesting. My mama grew her own eggplants, radishes, shallots, turnips, and bell peppers and green onions. We also planted and harvested okra, tomatoes, cucumbers, mustard greens, and cabbage. My mama would get her spices from the local grocery store and I used to enjoy watching my stepdad fill a jar with seasonings and then pickle our cucumbers, which always tasted so much better than store bought pickles. The jar was in the kitchen window and the sun would always shine on it. We would have to wait weeks for it to get ready. To this day, I try to plant vegetables with my children.

My mama and grandma always used fresh ingredients. I remember that the local fisherman came, the shrimp man came, or a hunter came and brought fresh meats like choupic, rabbit, and raccoon to our house. My grandparents also had chickens and hens that laid eggs. My stepdad fished and hunted as hobbies, and my mama and my brothers also loved to fish. But fishing wasn't my favorite thing to do as a family; I wasn't as good as my mama and my brothers.

I used to go pick fresh blackberries from the prickly bushes, but now you have to go and buy seeds or bushels of blackberries from the store. I don't see blackberry bushes as much as I used to as a child. We would pick these blackberries, put them in milk, cover them with sugar, and sneak outside to eat them. We were not allowed to go back into the house once we went outside, so going into the kitchen was a no-no. We would also eat the sugar cane from the sugarcane fields. My cousin would cut the sugar cane stalks and bring them to us and we would chew away in the adjacent field. We didn't have the privilege to eat sweets like candy and cakes at will. The sugar cane field was like our candy store since we couldn't get candy as much as we wanted to. I loved my childhood and my upbringing.

I was in charge of dicing the vegetables that I picked out of the garden. I remember sitting at the table with a bowl and towel, cutting okra with a butcher knife. I would cry when I cut the onions and my mama would take over when she could. She made all the meals—I was just her prep cook. My other kitchen duty was to rinse drain and add water to the rice. We ate rice all the time. My stepdad did not like rice, so my mom would cook him grits. Lots of fish and grits. I also had to stir the roux into the pot when she cooked gumbo while she was fixing up another dish or caring for one of my siblings. I was the oldest. They called me "Di" for short or "Dot." I was a "pot watcher." I can still hear their directions: "Don't burn my roux," "Keep stirring the pot." You could literally make a song out of these sentences based on the number of times I heard them during my kitchen duties.

My mama and grandma lived only two houses away. When they cooked, they cooked lots of food and our plates were very generous when they fed us. We had to eat all of our food, no matter what. We would eat in the house, but sometimes, we ate outside on the patio so that mom could keep her kitchen clean. Our dog, Toby, lived outside and, when I didn't want to eat all of my food, I gave it to him, so I wouldn't get fussed at by my mom.

My stepdad would be gone for two weeks at a time for work, but whenever he would come back home, we would have a big dinner that consisted of baked red fish, stuffed bell peppers, mac and cheese with a crawfish topping, mustard greens with turnips, candied yams, and eggplant rice dressing. All in one sitting! You would think it was a holiday when he came home from work.

Speaking of holidays, during those celebrations, we would either go to my grandmother's house or stay at home. My grandmother had eleven children. Two aunts lived around the corner and two of my uncles lived down the street. We lived in the same neighborhood, or "the hood," as some people call it. Everybody knew everybody and they all knew where the good food was. They were intimately acquainted with my mom's and grandmother's cooking. My grandmother makes the best red beans in the hood and sweet potato bread, especially for the holidays. Even today, when she gets a sweet tooth, she will go and pull out her sweet potato bread recipe.

Every so often, I would also visit my daddy and his family, and so, I'm no stranger to country life. When I visited them, I was awakened by crows or roosters every morning. My cousins on my paternal side also hunted and fished. My grandpa had a pet pot-belly pig that grew so huge, I didn't think it could move anymore. He cooked more than my paternal grandma. I must say that I am blessed to have had the opportunity to experience life with both my paternal grandparents and maternal grandparents, despite my mama not having a relationship with my father.

I didn't realize until later in life that I was being groomed to be a chef. I decided I would have my own business, because I wanted to be a role model for my children. Before that, I was in and out of jobs and hated the fact that an employer had some authority over how I could live my life. I had big dreams and other plans for how my life and its direction, but when my children came, it changed everything. My children became my first priority. Between military school and parenting, my life was chaotic, which threw me off of my original life plan.

But now, I am discovering my place in life and what my purpose is—I'm moving in an entirely different direction. Everything that happened in my upbringing as a child was God-ordained for me to be a chef and mama-preneur. I worship God in spirit and truth, so I'm not afraid to glorify God and all that He has done to bring me to this point in my life.

I hope these recipes spark up those childhood memories from mama's kitchen as well as help create your own memories. You'd be surprised by how much of an impact you can make in your family through cooking food. Stir the pot. Enjoy!

Mama's Kitchen

~~~~~

Lillie's Red Beans and Rice
Seafood Stuffed Bell Peppers
Baked Redfish
Creole Smothered Okra & Shrimp

LILLIE'S RED BEANS

Ingredients (7 servings)

9 ounces sausage, sliced

2 cups chopped onions

2 cups chopped green peppers

2 cups sliced celery

2 teaspoons minced garlic

2 bay leaves

2 teaspoons chopped parsley

1 pound Camellia dried beans sorted, soaked and cooked per package directions

1 tablespoon canola oil

1 (17 ounce) can chicken broth or water

2 teaspoon salt

2 teaspoon sugar

2 teaspoon Creole seasoning

1 teaspoon to taste ground black pepper

4 2/3 cups hot cooked rice

Directions

1. Add beans to stock pot or Dutch oven. Add chicken broth or water according to package directions. Bring mixture to a boil.

2. Coat hot saucepan with 1 tsp oil. Add all the vegetables, including garlic, and sauté for about 10 minutes, until they begin to brown.

3. Add sausage to pan. Cook for 5 to 8 minutes until well-browned.

4. Add sausage, Creole seasoning, black pepper and vegetables to bean mixture. Lower heat and simmer, covered, for about 45 minutes until the sauce is thick.

5. Stir in bay leaves, sugar, and parsley. Cook for 1 or 2 minutes more.

6. Discard bay leaves. Season to taste with Louisiana hot sauce (it's a southern thing!). Serve over rice.

SEAFOOD STUFFED BELL PEPPERS

Ingredients (7 Servings)

1 1/4 pound ground beef

1 pound shrimp, clean & peeled or crawfish tails

16 ounce Savoie's dressing mix

1 cup and 3 tablespoons beef stock

1 chopped onion

1 chopped green bell peppers

2 celery stalks, chopped

7 green bell peppers

2 1/4 (8 ounce) cans tomato sauce

1 tablespoon and 1/2 teaspoon Worcestershire sauce

1/4 teaspoon garlic powder

1/4 teaspoon onion powder

Salt and pepper to taste

1 1/4 teaspoons Italian seasoning

1 cup bread crumbs

Directions

1. Preheat oven to 350 degrees F (175 degrees C).

2. Add beef and the holy trinity seasoning (onion, bell peppers, celery) to Dutch oven. Cook the beef until evenly browned. Add Savoie's dressing mix. In a separate pan, sauté seafood in canola oil for 5 minutes, then add to beef mixture.

3. Remove and discard the tops, seeds, and inside membranes of the bell peppers. Rinse with water and dry peppers. Arrange peppers in a baking dish with the hollowed sides facing upward.

4. In the Dutch oven, mix the browned beef and seafood with beef stock, 1 can tomato sauce, Worcestershire sauce, garlic powder, onion powder, salt, and pepper. Spoon an equal amount of the mixture into each hollowed pepper. Mix the remaining tomato sauce and Italian seasoning in a bowl, and pour over the stuffed peppers. Sprinkle stuffed peppers with bread crumbs.

5. Cover with aluminum foil. Bake for 1 hour in the preheated oven until the peppers are tender.

BAKED REDFISH

Ingredients (4 to 6 Servings)

1 1/2 to 2 pounds fresh or frozen redfish fillets, thawed
1 teaspoon ground black pepper
1 teaspoon kosher salt
1/2 cups chopped onion
1/2 cups chopped celery
1 garlic clove, minced
2 1/2 cups canned tomatoes
2 cups tomato paste
1/4 cup melted butter or canola oil
Fresh parsley
1 lemon, sliced thin

Directions

1. Sauté onions, celery, and garlic in butter or oil. Cook for about 10 minutes and then add tomatoes and tomato paste. Cook, uncovered, over medium heat for 40 minutes, stirring occasionally. Add 1 cup of cold water and cook for 20 minutes.

2. Season fillets with salt and black pepper. Place in a baking dish and pour tomato mixture over the fish and bake at 325 degrees for 30 minutes, basting several times. Garnish with parsley and lemon slice.

CREOLE SMOTHERED OKRA WITH SHRIMP

Ingredients (Serves 6-8)

2 pounds okra, chopped
1 tablespoon oil
1 (16 ounce) can whole tomatoes, with juice
1 cup chopped onion
1/2 cup bell pepper, chopped
3/4 teaspoon chopped garlic
1 pound shrimp, peeled and deveined
1 pound sausage, sliced
1 tablespoon Creole Seasoning

Directions

1. Pour oil into the bottom of pan. Sauté onion, bell pepper and garlic until onion is clear.

2. Add okra and Creole seasoning cook until the okra is not slimy.

3. Add remaining ingredients.
4. Cover pot and simmer for 1 1/2 hours on low, stirring often.
5. Remove the cover for the last 10 minutes.

CHAPTER 2

Lessons Outside of Mama's Kitchen

"If you focus on what you left behind, you will never be able to see what lies ahead."

Ratatouille

My first year of high school began officially in the 10th grade. During my time in high school, Junior Reserve Officer Training Corps (JROTC) and food service were my electives. At the time, I chose those because they were of interest to me. I got more out of the classes than I expected. I became active in JROTC, participating in Color Guard and the rifle team and competing in state competitions. By doing so, I learned more than what the ordinary classroom taught me. I learned how to become a good team member, develop leadership skills, and accept failure with dignity. I developed a keen appreciation for the military. I was mesmerized by my experience and chose that elective for the rest of my high school career.

I chose food service as my second elective during eleventh grade. I wasn't interested in music or art, because I didn't think I was good at it. I also thought cooking would be easy for me since I had watched my mom and my grandmother cook. During this time, I became pregnant, something that happened because of my own lack of sexual education. I remember sitting in class, wondering what my teacher and my classmates would say about my enlarging belly. Then, I noticed that there was another student that sat in front of me and she was also pregnant. I still felt insecure, but knowing that we were experiencing the same problem brought me comfort. I had sympathy and empathy for her because of our similar plights.

Even though this pregnancy was unexpected, I never doubted that I would be able to finish school and join the military. This experience now helps me set an example of perseverance to my younger siblings and my own children. I realized that I was accountable for the lives of my siblings and my children and that helped me make better choices, while the reality of my personal struggle led them on better paths. They admire my courage and learn from my mistakes, so that they only repeat the things that enhance their lives. Even though the younger "me" did not always make good decisions, I was molded to become the person that I was supposed to be. It's not about the teen pregnancy—it's about what you do as a result of it.

So, quitting school was not an option—I was still focused on getting my diploma (and either way, my mama would have never let me quit). I learned that, no matter the circumstance, I still had to pursue my goals, and just because I may feel a certain way about myself, it did not mean that others felt the same way.

~~~~

My mama was a very strict parent and did an excellent job raising me to be respectful and obedient. I was a good student in school. Certain things I didn't learn at home, I learned in there. My mama always taught us by showing us; there weren't any step-by-step directions other than a list on the kitchen table of the chores we had to do that day. I also learned how to follow recipes in the food service class, which helped me better follow directions and respect leadership later on in my military career.

More than anything else, I learned to be patient with myself. I didn't always get it right the first time while cooking and I still don't always get it right the first time. I learned to pray and ask for patience. Cooking outside of my mama's kitchen, I began appreciating other perspectives and ways of doing things. It broadened my appreciation for using diverse ways to accomplish a goal and opened the door to my appetite and curiosity regarding other cuisines and ways of doing things in the kitchen.

I looked forward to cooking in class, those memories still being some of my most cherished high school experiences. My anticipation of going to this class and the new things I learned helped me weather the storm of my unexpected pregnancy. I remember one day making my first King Cake. I suddenly found that I could do things that I've never done before, just by trying. I got a good grade on the final product and I was so proud that I wished I could take the cake home to my mama. But instead, we took turns sharing and tasting each other's King Cake. Everyone's cake came out perfect, and we all got the King Cake right on the first try. It must be a Louisiana thing!

My senior year was refreshing. Because of support from my family, I was able to go back to school with a clean slate and finish without the responsibility of being a new mom hindering me in any way. My friends were still the same and I began moving towards my goal of joining the military.

I got my first job as a caterer for a big food service corporation. I worked late hours for minimum wage, which was only $4.25 back then, but I had a great experience. I didn't cook much at my job. I mostly prepped food, and set and bussed tables. I had no idea at the time that what I was learning would lead me to my chosen career or my current business venture. The valuable lesson I learned is that, if you're happy with what you do, the pay is only icing on the cake, experience is your real salary. I had no complaints with my first job, and I was blessed and fortunate to have my mama to help me with my daughter.

~~~~~

I continued in my final year in ROTC and resumed my duties as a student in JROTC. Initially, I applied to enlist while in my senior high school, but I was told by my recruiter that, because I was underage, I needed my mother's consent. Additionally, it was impossible to enlist without signing my daughter's guardian rights over to my mother. I declined. I felt I was not emotionally ready to do that. Still, I dreamed of enlisting in the military and made that happen for myself.

I joined the Army National Guard, because of my experience in Army JROTC. I was interested in learning more. I wanted to do something different and go to new and exciting places. At the time, the benefits of the National Guard worked better for my circumstances, since I got education benefits and training. In my mind, I could do my basic training and advanced individual training (AIT) and return home for one weekend during one-month training and be a parent to my children. About the same time, my first marriage to my baby's father ended—we had married two years after graduating high school, but things did not work out. Even though my entrance into the army came with all of these complications, I would not trade my military experience and deployment for anything else. I gained so much from that phase of my journey. In fact, that was how I met my current, wonderful husband.

I entered into AIT at the Quartermaster School in Ft. Lee Virginia as a 92G Food Service Specialist. Food service is the morale backbone of a fighting force and combat multiplier. As the former Director ACES LTC Vtipil often said, "Army Food Service touches more soldiers on a daily basis than any other MOS in the Army." I knew my work was crucial to the success of any unit and I had an awesome experience. I was surrounded by like-minded soldiers who either loved to cook or had no other choice but to learn to love to cook. I learned the ins and outs of a commercial kitchen. We wore "cook whites," the term we used to describe our uniforms when we cooked in the dining facility (DFAC). It was a white shirt and white pants, and we were expected to keep them white throughout our entire work shift, since a cook is expected to be clean; as they say, cleanliness is closest to godliness. This was one of my first lessons: safe food service and sanitation. During formation, before we started anything, we had an inspection called a cooks mount. Our hair, nails, uniform, any unauthorized jewelry were inspected: "Dress right dress, hands out." I had already learned from my mama and grandma to keep the kitchen clean at all times and to always wash my hands, but it was reinforced at AIT.

Our military occupational specialty training consisted of classroom training, practical training, and army warrior training. As simple as boiling an egg may seem, there is a technique. In the military, there is a technical manual (TM) for everything. We followed TM recipe preparation and serving standards. I learned the basics of food and cooking such as about weights and measurements, nutrients, knife safety, utensils, and sanitation. I remember our class instruction working in the DFAC. We were put into teams to prepare, cook, and set the line for active duty soldiers. Our team had the responsibility of baking biscuits. I will never forget when

I turned the switch on the commercial mixer and flour exploded everywhere. It was so embarrassing! But since then, I always check the mixer properly for the correct setting before turning it on.

The main job of a food service specialist is to serve high quality, nutritious, and appealing food. To do so, you must be able to follow recipes, perform each skill correctly, and accurately weigh and measure all ingredients. The primary reason for recipes is standardized cooking. When serving a menu item or food product, consistency is the key. When I'm cooking for my family, I rarely use recipes unless it is my first time making a dish. After I learn how to cook the dish, I can adjust it according to my taste. But there is a first time for everything.

I needed these recipes in military training and culinary school, because I had never made the dishes prior to my experience as a military cook. I learned that moist heat cooking and dry heat cooking were broad terms for how food is cooked. Moist heat cooking is when liquid is used outside of the food and dry heat is when no fluid is used. In my mama's kitchen, there were general terms used like stew, smothered, baked, or fried. During AIT, that knowledge increased and everything came incredibly naturally to me. I graduated in the top five of my 2003 class. Being an honor graduate had its benefits in AIT: I had the opportunity to attend a dinner with top officials, since I was afforded the privilege of being one of the top two soldiers in the class. It was an extraordinary experience for me; the food was presented by Army and Marine food service specialists who worked in the Pentagon, professionals who rival some of the top chefs in America. There were dishes I'd never imagined existed or tasted before.

It's a Louisiana Thing!

~~~~

Baked Gouda Cheese Grits
Southern Fried Catfish
Seafood Sauce Picante
Mardi Gras King Cake

BAKED GOUDA CHEESE GRITS

Ingredients (6 servings)

2 quarts water
2 cups grits
1 tablespoon salt
6 ounces Gouda cheese
1/4 pound butter
3 cloves garlic, minced
3 eggs, beaten
2 cups milk

Directions

1. Add grits to boiling salted water and cook. Cover for about 20 minutes, until grits are tender, but still creamy.

2. Remove from heat and add cheese, garlic, and butter. Stir until cheese and butter are melted.

3. Cool, then add eggs and milk. Pour into a greased casserole and bake 325 degrees for 50 minutes.

SOUTHERN FRIED CATFISH

Ingredients (6 servings)

2 1/2 cups flour
1 1/2 cups yellow cornmeal
1 teaspoon salt
1 teaspoon pepper
1 teaspoon cayenne pepper
1 teaspoon garlic salt
1/2 cup parsley, chopped
2 pounds catfish filets
Oil for frying

Directions

1. Combine flour, corn meal, seasonings, and parsley.

2. Season catfish and dip in corn meal mixture. Shake off excess.

3. Fry in hot oil at 375 degrees until golden brown. Drain on paper towels.

SEAFOOD SAUCE PICANTE

Ingredients (Serves 6-8)

1 pound fish fillets (cut into pieces)
1 pound shrimp, (peeled and deveined)
1 pound lump crab meat
4 Tablespoon cooking oil
2 medium onions, chopped
1 can tomato paste
1 can diced tomatoes
1/2 teaspoon sugar
1/2 cup chopped bell pepper
1/2 cup finely chopped celery
1 cup water
2 Tablespoon finely chopped garlic
4 Tablespoon chopped parsley
1/2 cup green onion, chopped
Salt and pepper to taste

Directions

1. Sauté finely chopped onions in oil. Add tomato paste. Cook until fat rises.

2. Add sugar and continue cooking for about 5 minutes.

3. Add bell peppers, celery and garlic. Stir well, then add water and cook for 1 hour over slow fire.

4. Add diced tomatoes, green onion, parsley and chunks of fish and shrimp. Salt and pepper. Cover and cook slowly for 1/2 hour.

5. Add lump crab meat.

6. Serve over rice.

MARDI GRAS KING CAKE

Ingredients (10 servings)

1 (16-ounce) container sour cream
1/3 cup sugar
1/4 cup butter
1 teaspoon salt
2 (1/4-ounce) envelopes active dry yeast
1/2 cup warm water 100 to 110 degrees
1 tablespoon sugar
2 large eggs, lightly beaten
6 to 6 1/2 cups bread flour
1/3 cup butter, softened
1/2 cup sugar
1 1/2 teaspoons ground cinnamon
Creamy Glaze
Purple-, green-, and gold- sugar sprinkles

Directions

1. Cook first four ingredients in a medium saucepan over low heat, stirring often, until butter melts. Set aside and cool mixture to 100° to 110°.

2. Stir together yeast, 1/2 cup warm water, and 1 tablespoon sugar in a 1-cup glass measuring cup; let stand for 5 minutes.

3. Beat sour cream mixture, yeast mixture, eggs, and 2 cups flour at medium speed with a heavy-duty electric stand mixer until smooth. Reduce speed to low, and gradually add enough of the remaining flour (4 to 4 1/2 cups) until a soft dough forms.

4. Turn dough out onto a lightly floured surface; knead until smooth and elastic (about 10 minutes). Place in a well-greased bowl, turning to grease top. Cover and let rise in a warm place (85°), free from drafts, for 1 hour or until dough is doubled in bulk.

5. Punch down dough, and divide in half. Roll each portion into a 22- x 12-inch rectangle. Spread 1/3 cup softened butter evenly on each rectangle, leaving a 1-inch border. Stir together 1/2 cup sugar and cinnamon, and sprinkle evenly over butter on each rectangle.

6. Roll up each dough rectangle, jelly-roll fashion, starting at one long side. Place one dough roll, seam side down, on a lightly greased baking sheet. Bring ends of roll together to form an oval ring, moistening and pinching edges together to seal. Repeat with second dough roll. Cover and let rise in a warm place (85°), free from drafts, for 20 to 30 minutes or until doubled in bulk.

7. Bake at 375° for 14 to 16 minutes or until golden. Slightly cool cakes on pans on wire racks (about 10 minutes). Drizzle Creamy Glaze evenly over warm cakes; sprinkle with colored sugars, alternating colors and forming bands. Let cool completely.

CHAPTER 3

Journey into the Real World of Cooking

"The only real stumbling block is fear of failure. In cooking, you've got to have a 'what the hell attitude.'"

—Julia Child

I was in the military for nine years and most of that time was spent cooking. It was a great way to start my culinary career. After an eighteen-month deployment, I eventually decided to go to culinary school with the help of my husband. It just seemed like a natural fit. At that time, I was in Thibodaux, Louisiana and began attending Chef John Folse Culinary Institute at Nicholls State University for their two-year program. I heard about the program before my entering the military and it was named after a famous chef who actually taught one of my classes.

I entered culinary school with an open mind and an eager attitude to learn, and it turned out to be a very positive experience. I looked forward to baking class, because baking was a challenge. I didn't bake much at home, so I always wanted to learn. I was amazed at the culinary creations I baked. We made puff pastry swans, brioche, chocolate mousse, and panna cotta. Baking is about precision and knowing mathematics is essential. Baking was a struggle I overcame every time I entered the culinary baking kitchen.

When I got into practicals and we did knife skills, we had a test on how to cut vegetables to a certain standard. I was always afraid of the knife skills tests, because one of my instructors would always say, "If you don't cut your finger at least one time, you are not doing it right." I did end up cutting my finger, so I felt almost relieved after that—I figured that I'd gotten my "one" out of the way.

We also participated in a student-run restaurant that was open to the public and was recognized in the community for its excellent food and service. I had an opportunity to serve as maître de and captain in the front of the house and back: I prepped, cooked, washed dishes, everything. I also found new camaraderie amongst the culinary students and instructors, as well as strengthened our bond.

~~~~~

This choice to go to culinary school came after three kids and the fact that both my husband and I were still in the military; however, this decision was good for my family dynamic. When I started culinary school, I learned how to cook new cuisines such as plantains, cous cous, quinoa, and Lobster Thermidor. These were very different types of food from our occasional southern or soul food of okra gumbo, chitterlings (which my husband dislikes), or smothered pork chops. My husband has always loved my cooking since the day we met, and it didn't hurt to learn better techniques in cooking—like the saying goes, "The way to a man's heart is through his stomach." So my husband was excited to try the food I learned to cook. His palate and taste buds even changed a little. We started going to different restaurants and order something new and different every time. He always says he has an awesome wife, because I know how to read and order from even the most complex, foreign menus and I even taught him some culinary terms. He is as proud of my culinary knowledge and of me as I am proud of his accomplishments. He is now a "food expert" whenever there is a conversation about food in his social circles. He proudly shares what he has garnered from my experience as a chef with others.

I wish to take a moment to say that, truly, my greatest fan and spiritual influence currently comes from my husband. He is a godly man and imparts wisdom in my life. Although I can be stubborn sometimes and I don't want to accept what he is saying, I know that he is truthful and wise when I ask for advice. When I nearly gave up on pursuing my passion, my husband persuaded me to get back on the right track and he was my greatest cheerleader. Because he believed in me, I was not going to disappoint him or me, because I wanted to show him that our conversation was meaningful. He was right in telling me the hard truth. In my heart, I knew I should've gone to culinary school sooner, but I didn't want to tell him that at that time, now he knows. God has graced both my husband and me to make mistakes, be forgiven, and move on. When you burn the roux while making gumbo, toss it out and start over.

By the time I was in my senior year of culinary school, I was pregnant with my fourth child. I had early mornings and late nights during that semester. I ended up having to go to the emergency room, because I was having stomach pains, probably due to the long hours, and my chef instructor went with me. I stayed in the hospital for one night and received fluids for dehydration. My culinary chef instructors were very supportive and concerned. Because of the numerous hours we spent together, the family I found in the culinary school was similar to the experience I had in the military.

Still, school did not come without its difficulties. Because of this pregnancy, I knew I could not immediately go into the workforce. I began to wonder about my rationale for attending school in the first place and became despondent. I felt like I just couldn't be it all—a super mom and an awesome chef. I decided to take additional courses to broaden my experience and skills. I even ventured outside of my career path and took classes to become a teacher, but I soon realized that it was not what I was passionate about. I loved teaching and felt some fulfillment from it, but it didn't allow me to pursue my ultimate dream of owning a catering business.

In addition to struggling with my own decisions and circumstances, my mother passed. She had battled cancer, getting medical treatments and focusing on spending time with her grandkids. Neither my family, including my grandmother, knew much about my experience in culinary school. I was afraid they might say, "Why does she need to go to culinary school? We taught her how to cook!" I knew they wouldn't understand the bigger picture. My oldest brother even told me I should go to school to become a lawyer. I thought about it, but I had other plans.

I continued working towards my goals and my delayed entry into the career that I love turned out to be a blessing of sorts: it allowed me to be a mama and lay a solid foundation for my children. I learned more lessons in life through this experience than I can actually tell in the pages of this book. I got a lot of practical hands-on training, during which I was able to make mistakes and learn from them, all under the supervision of my instructors. If I burned the bread, I could start over and do it differently. But by far, my greatest accomplishment was actually getting my degree. I was the first and only one of my siblings to get a degree. I learned, once again, that I could do anything if I just put forth the effort.

I am now able to pursue my catering business without

regrets. I once considered opening a restaurant, but it seemed too structured and my first love in entrepreneurship was catering. I think it goes with my personality: I like to serve and meet people's needs in an informal setting. Formal is excellent too, but people can relax and enjoy the fun at event venues. I also wanted to become an entrepreneur, because of the freedom it provides me with, I felt that my gifts and talents could be shared with the world based on my own terms and core values. I believe in the spirit of entrepreneurship and leaving a legacy for my family, teaching my children that they are in an environment where they can learn and progress in. And although I like to take the reins, I also know the value of learning from others. I love what other perspectives can bring to the table and what an enhancing mutual relationship can add to individual wealth of each other.

I love being able to fulfill my passion with purpose. Owning a catering business had been a dream of mine for almost ten years and I could not sit on it any longer. It wouldn't leave me alone. When you are destined to do something, it won't leave you alone until you pay attention!

Culinary School Classics

~~~~~

Spinach Quiche Lorraine
Brioche
Ratatouille
Chicken Marsala

SPINACH QUICHE LORRAINE

Ingredients (7 servings)

1 cup shredded gruyere cheese

1/4 cup onion, finely diced

1/2 pound fresh mushrooms, chopped

1 Tablespoon butter

3 slices bacon, cooked and crumbled

16 ounces fresh spinach, stems removed (Or 1 package frozen spinach thawed and squeezed dry)

4 eggs, beaten slightly

2 cups heavy cream

Salt and pepper to taste

1 pinch of cayenne pepper

1 pinch of grated fresh nutmeg

1 10-inch pie crust

Directions

1. Preheat oven to 425 degrees. Rub butter over surface of the unbaked pie shell. Bake pie shell for 10 minutes. Remove.

2. In a medium skillet, melt butter over medium heat. Sauté mushrooms and onion in butter until lightly browned. Set aside.

3. Combine eggs, cream, salt, pepper, nutmeg, and cayenne pepper. Beat just long enough to mix thoroughly. Blend in mushrooms and onions.

4. Sprinkle pie shell with crumbled bacon, spinach, and cheese. Pour in cream mixture.

5. Bake at 400 degrees F for 10 minutes.

6. Reduce heat to 350 degrees F and bake for another 40 minutes or until set.

BRIOCHE

(Adapted from *Professional Baking*)

Ingredients (7 servings)

2-ounce milk
1/2-ounce yeast, fresh
2 ounce bread flour
5 ounce eggs
8 ounce bread flour
1/2 ounce sugar
1 teaspoon salt
7 ounce butter, softened

Method to Know

Sponge method: Procedures are done in two stages:

1. 1. Combine part or all of the liquid, all of the yeast, and part of the flour (and sometimes part of the sugar). Mix into a soft dough and let ferment until double in bulk.

2. 2. Fold or punch down and add the rest of the flour and the remaining ingredients. Mix to a uniform and smooth dough

Directions

1. Scald the milk and cool to lukewarm. Dissolve the yeast. Add the flour and mix to make a sponge. Let rise until double.

2. Gradually mix in the eggs and then dry the ingredients using the paddle attachment to make a soft dough.

3. Beat in the butter a little at a time until it is completely absorbed and the dough is smooth. Dough will be very soft and sticky

Tip: If the dough requires much handling in makeup, such as for small brioche rolls, it is easiest to retard the dough overnight. Making it up while chilled reduces stickiness. If the dough is simply put into pans, the stickiness and softness is not a problem and does not need to be retarded. Ferment for 20 minutes. Scale and pan.

4. For a small brioche, roll the dough in a round piece

5. Using the edge of your hand, pinch off about ¼ of the dough without breaking it apart. Roll the dough on the table so both parts are round.

6. Place the dough in the pan, large end first. With your fingertips, press smaller ball into the larger ball.

7. Egg wash after proofing.

8. Bake 400 degrees F for small rolls.

RATATOUILLE

Ingredients (8-10 servings)

1/2 cup olive oil
1 eggplant, washed and cut, with skin on, into 1-inch cubes
3 medium zucchini washed, ends removed, cut in 1-inch cubes
3 small onions, cut into 1-inch cubes
3 green bell peppers washed, seeded, and cut into 1-inch squares
5 ripe tomatoes; peeled, seeded and coarsely cubed
6 cloves garlic; peeled, crushed, and minced
1/2 cup water
2 teaspoons salt
1/2 teaspoon freshly ground black pepper

Directions

1. Heat 1/4 cup of the oil in large skillet.

2. Sauté the eggplant cubes for about 8 minutes. Remove with slotted spoon and transfer to a large, heavy flameproof casserole. Then, sauté the zucchini cubes until browned for about 8 minutes. Then transfer to the casserole.

3. Add about 1/4 cup more oil to the pan and sauté the onions and peppers together for about 6 minutes. Add them to the casserole.

4. Add the tomatoes, garlic, water, salt, and pepper to the casserole and bring to a boil over medium heat. Reduce heat, cover, and cook over low heat for 1 hour.

5. Remove the cover, increase the heat to medium, and cook for another 20 minutes, uncovered, to reduce some of the liquid. Stir once in a while to prevent scorching.

6. Let rest for 30 minutes before serving.

CHICKEN MARSALA

Ingredients (4 servings)

4 6-ounce skinless, boneless chicken breast halves, pounded 1/2 in thickness

4 teaspoons all-purpose flour, divided

3/4 teaspoon salt, divided

1/4 teaspoon freshly ground black pepper

2 tablespoons olive oil, divided

1/2 cup chopped onion

1/4 teaspoon crushed red pepper

5 garlic cloves, thinly sliced

1 1/2 cups thinly sliced shiitake mushroom caps

1/2 cup thinly sliced portabella mushrooms

1 1/2 cups thinly sliced button mushrooms

1 teaspoon dried oregano

1/2 cup dry Marsala wine

2/3 cup chicken broth

1/4 cup small fresh basil leaves

Directions

1. In a bowl or plate, combine and mix together flour with salt, black pepper, and oregano. Dredge the chicken on both sides with flour mixture.

2. Heat a large stainless steel skillet over medium-high heat. Add 1 tablespoon oil to pan and coat the pan. Add chicken. Cook for 3 minutes on each side or until done. Remove from pan. Cover and keep warm.

3. Add an additional tablespoon of butter to pan. Add shallots, garlic, and mushrooms to pan. Cook until mushrooms are softened and browned, stirring frequently.

4. With heat remaining, add 1 tablespoon oil to pan over medium-high heat. Add onion, red pepper, and garlic. Sauté for 2 minutes or until onion is lightly browned. Add remaining 1/2 teaspoon salt, portabella, shiitake, button mushrooms, and oregano. Sauté for 6 minutes or until mushrooms release moisture and darken.

5. Add remaining 1 teaspoon flour and cook for 1 minute, stirring constantly. Stir in wine. Add broth and bring to a boil.

6. Reduce heat, and simmer for 1 minute. Add chicken and cook for 2 minutes or until thoroughly heated, turning chicken once.

7. Garnish with basil.

CHAPTER 4

Uncovering My Passion for Cooking

"If you can't figure out your purpose, figure out your passion. For your passion will lead you right into your purpose."

Bishop T. D. Jakes

Some of my most memorable moments in cooking are of the responses that I've received from people who ate my culinary creations, the satisfaction they derive from what I cook.

After my mama passed, I moved into our family home for a few months, living with two of my sisters and two of my brothers. I was home most of the time, so it seemed as though I was the mother hen. I cooked for everybody. I made dishes that my mama used to make: red beans, macaroni and cheese, and smothered okra. Every now and then, I would send a plate over to my mama's friend and neighbor, because it was something he looked forward to when my mama was living. She always cooked for her family and share with him too.

I have so many memories of cooking for others, too many to talk about; all of those experiences would probably fit into another book. Here is the recipe I used to follow in order to uncover my true passion:

Ingredients:

Thoughts: creative and positive

Lifetime of Experiences: from conception to current

Lifelong Learner: having a never-ending pursuit of education

Skills: tested and approved

God-given talents: those things that come naturally to you and you would do then for free

Everyday Life Challenges: professional and personal that mold and shape you for excellence

Directions:

1. Take inventory: I first looked over my life experiences and considered my skills, my talents, my education, and challenges that I'd faced in life.

2. Let your thoughts simmer: I needed to be in the right mindset, since my thoughts created my atmosphere. I couldn't move to the next step of actually pressing forward in life or cooking without changing my thinking from not being able to pursue my dreams as a mama to doing anything with the help of God. In cooking, this is the prep work with all ingredients. In cooking terms, it is called *mise en place*, a French term for making advance preparations and putting everything in place. This is an important step for having an effective operational kitchen.

3. Start using the ingredients: I decided that my experiences in culinary started when I was a little girl growing up in my mother's home, then my education in high school, later in military occupational school, and finally in culinary school. I know I would still need more education to hone my craft and skills. In cooking, if the knife is not sharp, you can cut yourself more easily. In other words, you are better off perfecting your skills versus working with what you got. Now, I knew that I needed education. It was much easier for me to follow

my passion, since education gave me the tools I needed to be successful.

4. Begin with determination and trust in yourself: Overcoming challenges is like measuring quantities to the exact ounce required for a particular dish. In life, the challenge for me was parenting and reaching my career and educational goals.

5. Gather all your experiences, skills, and talents, mixed with a little faith the size of a mustard seed: I started stirring the gifts inside of me. I didn't stop. I looked for a way to move around problems.

I know that cooking is my passion, because almost every experience in my life led me to where I am now. No matter what ingredient I left out or added, I still feel the same way about cooking and serving others. I always want to add to my life, so I feel inspired when I'm serving others and sharing my gifts and talents. Food service helps me do that. There was a time when it didn't matter if I got paid for my services and I still feel that way in certain instances. When I'm cooking for my church or charity/nonprofit organizations, my passion for what I am providing for these entities is far greater than the monetary value.

I use my gifts to serve others and my family. I help others plan parties, because what's the point of celebrating if you don't have food? Being able to share my cooking talents with others brings me great joy knowing that it serves a God-given purpose. I'm happy when I walk in my purpose. I'm happy when I make pumpkin cheesecake or shrimp and grits and others are satisfied by it and create happy memories while partaking in my culinary creation.

Cooking is not only my passion, it's my ministry.

Fellowship & Food

~~~~~

Shrimp and Sausage Jambalaya
Pumpkin Pecan Cheesecake
Pickled Okra & Shrimp Salad
Hoppin John

SHRIMP AND SAUSAGE JAMBALAYA

Ingredients (4 -6 servings)

2 tbsp. butter

8 oz. Andouille sausage, or other spicy smoked sausage, sliced 1/4" thick

2 tbsp. paprika

1 tbsp. ground cumin

1/2 tsp cayenne pepper

1/2 tsp fresh ground black pepper

1/2 tsp garlic powder

1 tsp salt

1/2 cup diced tomato, fresh or canned

1 large green bell pepper, diced

2 ribs celery, sliced 1/4" thick

4 green onions, sliced thin

1 cup rice

3 cups chicken broth

1 pound large shrimp, peeled and deveined

Directions

1. In a heavy bottomed pot or cast iron with a lid, melt the butter over medium heat. Add the sliced sausage and cook, stirring for 5 minutes. Add the paprika, cumin, cayenne, black pepper, and salt. Sauté the spices for 1 minute and then add the tomatoes. Cook stirring for a few minutes to let some of the liquid from the tomatoes evaporate. Add the green bell pepper, celery, and most of the green onions (reserve some of the dark green slices of the onions to garnish the top). Cook, stirring for 5 minutes.

2. Stir in the rice and mix well. Add the stock, turn the heat up to high, and bring to a simmer. Reduce the heat to low, cover the pot, and cook for 20 minutes.

3. When the rice is tender, add the shrimp, stir in, and cook covered for 5 minutes. Taste for seasoning and adjust if needed. Serve the jambalaya in bowls with green onions sprinkled on top.

PUMPKIN PECAN CHEESECAKE

Ingredients (8 servings)

For the Topping
1/2 cup firmly packed light brown sugar
5 tablespoons butter, chilled
1 1/2 cups chopped pecans

For the Cheesecake
1 1/2 cups graham cracker crumbs
3/4 cup firmly packed light brown sugar
3/4 cup sugar
5 large eggs
6 tablespoons butter, melted
3 (8 ounce) packages cream cheese, room temperature
1/2 cup whipping cream
1 can pumpkin puree
1/2 teaspoon nutmeg
1/2 teaspoon cinnamon
1/4 teaspoon clove

Directions

1. For topping: Place sugar in small bowl. Add butter and cut in until mixture resembles coarse meal. Stir in pecans and set aside.

2. For cheesecake: Blend crumbs, ¼ cup sugar, and butter in bowl.

3. Press into bottom and up sides of 9-inch diameter spring form pan. Chill.

4. Preheat oven to 350 degrees F (165C).

5. Beat cream cheese until smooth. Mix in white and brown sugars. Chill.

6. Preheat oven to 350 degrees F (165C).

7. Beat cream cheese until smooth. Mix in white and brown sugars. Add eggs, one at a time, and beat until fluffy. Blend in pumpkin, cream and spices. Pour into crust.

8. Bake until center no longer moves when pan is shaken (about 1 ½ hours).

9. Sprinkle pecan topping over cheesecake. Bake for 15 minutes longer.

10. Cool. Cover and refrigerate overnight.

PICKLED OKRA SALAD & SHRIMP

Ingredients (6 servings)

1 (3-oz.) package boil-in-bag shrimp-and-crab boil

1 1/2 pounds peeled and deveined, medium-size raw shrimp (3 1/40 count)

1/2 cup sliced pickled okra

1 (4-oz.) jar diced pimiento, drained

1/3 cup mayonnaise

3 tablespoons minced red onion

1/2 teaspoon lime zest

3 tablespoons fresh lime juice

1/4 teaspoon pepper

1/8 teaspoon salt

3 large avocados, sliced

1 head Romaine lettuce

Directions

1. Bring 8 cups water to a boil in a 3-qt. saucepan. add crab boil, and cook for 5 minutes. Add shrimp. Cover, remove from heat, and let stand for 10 minutes or just until shrimp turn pink. Drain and cool for 10 minutes.

2. Meanwhile, combine pickled okra, diced pimiento, mayonnaise, red onion, lime zest, lime juice, pepper, and salt. Add shrimp, and serve immediately with avocado slices on Romaine lettuce, or cover and chill until ready to serve.

HOPPIN' JOHN

Ingredients (8-10 servings)

1 pound package dry black eyed peas
3/4 cup ham, bacon or sausage, chopped and cooked
1 medium onion, diced
2 cloves garlic, minced
1 cup bell pepper, chopped
1 cup celery, diced
1 cup tomatoes, diced
1 teaspoon Cajun seasoning
1/2 teaspoon ground Thyme
1/2 teaspoon ground cumin
1/2 teaspoon black pepper
6 cups chicken stock
2 Tablespoons canola oil –
2 cups long grain white rice, cooked

Instructions

1. In a 6-quart soup pot, heat the canola oil on medium high heat. Sauté the onion, bell pepper, garlic and celery until the onion is tender.

2. Add chicken stock. Add the tomatoes, seasonings, ham, and black eyed peas.

3. Bring to a boil. Lower heat to medium low and cover. Simmer for one hour or until peas are tender, stirring occasionally. Check frequently and add water if needed to keep covered in liquid.

4. During the last 1/2 hour of cooking the peas, cook rice according to the package directions.

5. Spoon out some rice in a deep bowl. Cover generously with the Hoppin' John and serve hot with cornbread.

CHAPTER 5

Challenging Life Lessons

"The only thing predictable about life is its unpredictability."

Ratatouille

I had three distinct opportunities to *not* fulfill my purpose: I got into an unsuitable relationship and married too soon, became a pharmacy technician, and I went back to school to become a teacher. During my first marriage, I was unhappy, because I knew my life was for fulfilling my hopes and dreams, not to justify my situation. But I had a baby and I thought that I had to be married to her father and have a family, and this vision was at the forefront of my future. I grew up believing in family structure, living in a home with both my mother and father. I knew it was the right and good thing to do, but I soon realized that it wasn't the God thing to do for my life. Just because I was in a relationship with my child's father didn't mean it was ordained by God. I'm thankful for those lessons and that I was eventually able to move on to my destiny and fulfill my purpose.

Although I couldn't join the military out of high school once I was married, there was little hindering me from enlisting. It was an easy decision, considering that I quickly realized that my first marriage was not the right choice. It still worked out for my good: by joining the military, I was able to pursue my goals and become a food service specialist. In honesty, when I was offered the job as a military cook, I wasn't too fond of it because it didn't seem trendy and I was unaware of my calling and purpose. My thoughts soon changed when I noticed how much the other military personnel appreciated military cooks—everybody has to eat. After a long day of work or training in the Army, soldiers look forward to showing up at the chow hall (DFAC). I was also watching the clock and counting down to chow time. This revelation catapulted me into my purpose.

After my Operation Iraqi Freedom deployment, I continued my studies as a pharmacy technician, graduated, and became employed in a hospital pharmacy. I had personal challenges and difficulties meeting the job demands and simultaneously being a mother. By this time, I'd become engaged to my present, awesome husband. Soon, I decided to let go and let God work it out. I had previous evidence of Him working faithfully in my life for my good. So, I started to wonder why I was trying to do this on my own. The twelve-hour shift in the pharmacy was not ideal for me. During that time, I also became a Mary Kay consultant, another unfulfilling line of work. I had no interest in selling makeup. I had no joy there.

I felt joy slowly show back up in my life and my purpose resurface when, after a couple conversations with my husband, I enrolled at Nicholls State University. I attended class, learned cooking techniques, and actually cooked, feeling comfortable as I did during my AIT (Army Career Training Program). In the military, I found out that pain hurts only for a few seconds, but it is soon over. There were many times that I wanted to quit doing sit-ups, I wanted to quit the push-ups, but the motivation from the drill sergeant wouldn't allow me to. In life, there were also times I wanted to give up, but my passion was still burning inside me and my purpose was still waiting to be fulfilled. I learned never to quit. The stress may be present, but I have something on the inside of me that enables me to endure. Both the military and culinary school strengthened my discipline, tenacity, and obedience. Instead of saying, "Yes, drill sergeant," I was saying, "Yes, Chef." Professional cooking is hard work, but it's rewarding for me.

As the saying goes, "If you can't take the heat, get out of the kitchen."

~~~~~

Cooking and serving food gives me great satisfaction. Every moment I in the kitchen, preparing food for my family and then sharing it with them, makes me feel good. They enjoy the food, fun, and fellowship, while I get to make fancy cuisines like beef Wellington, escargot, and foie gras to impress my family. I also like to surprise them with a gourmet culinary creation like scallops with asparagus, parmesan risotto, and strawberry salad for Valentine's Day.

When I think of these times with my family, I am so glad that I did not give up when circumstances were not what I expected them to be, because it has always been about my family. In high school, my grandmother had the most influence on me. She still has some of that influence in my life as a married woman, and she is my heart. She was a rock during the earlier parts of my life and a blessing to my generation. I always wanted to impress her and always felt more comfortable talking to my grandma than I was my mama. My grandma knows almost everything about me. Then, when I enlisted in the military, my kids were my greatest influences. I wanted to return home to a proud parent and make my time away from them worthwhile. I wasn't thinking about any other outside influences. I wanted to do my best and be a success and I was. Then, when I had insecurities about my chosen college major, my husband reassured me that it was not a waste of time. He became just as interested as I was to learn more about culinary arts—he is now my food critic and tastes all my experimental creations.

Even though I was blessed to have such a wonderful connection to all my family, I felt that I was so much more than a mother and a housewife. And yet, the demands of a culinary career made it seem almost impossible for me to work and care for my children. Since my parents, as well as my husband's, passed away, my family no longer has relatives close by to assist us. It also wasn't feasible for me to pay childcare expenses while I worked outside of the home. This was tough and unsettling for me, but I still decided to return back to school. My intentions were to have a career that worked around my children's school schedule. I even started working towards an alternative teacher certification. I became a substitute teacher and enjoyed teaching, but once again, I was not interested in the subject matter and I was not able to pursue my dreams of becoming an entrepreneur. Once more, I was being pushed into my purpose.

God will take you where you need to be, the path you belong on. But just because I ventured off and did things my way did not mean I was not supposed to go there. Every encounter was meant to show me the right direction. I needed those experiences to confirm my destiny, reignite my passion, and lead me to my purpose. Experiences are better than anything you learn, because of the wisdom received from it. I remember, when I was younger, my mama told me not to touch the hot pot on the stove. Well, I wanted to taste the food before it was done. I could tell from seeing the red flames, feeling the heat, and observing the steam flowing in the atmosphere, that it was hot. But I decided I would just be extremely careful. Initially, when I took the lid off the pot without using a potholder, it burned my fingers. The steam from the pot scorched my face a little, and when I put the spoon in my mouth and tasted it, I burned my tongue. Yes, my mother told me not to do it, but I had to experience it for myself in order to learn the lesson. I will never forget that day. I now know experiences can be life-changing and you carry that wisdom learned with you for the rest of your life.

In this way, God distinctly showed me what my purpose was by allowing me to have hardships and challenges to learn from my mistake, and now I can also teach others. As a parent, I can provide the guidance my children will need. I can share my experiences and others can learn from them. I try to remain teachable, and give both honor and respect where they are due. My primary purpose is to give back and be of service to others with a willing and humble spirit. When cooking food, you are sharing and giving something of yourself. Food heals. Food comforts. Food is nourishment. When I am serving others, I am also serving God. I am sacrificing my time, efforts, and love to comfort and satisfy someone's need. Being obedient to His will is better than making unproductive sacrifices.

~~~~~

In AIT, I had positive experiences such as dining with top military officials and receiving a coin of appreciation from an Air Force three-star general. Military coins are usually embellished with a brightly colored design, which is a tribute to a particular unit in a military. When they are received from a superior officer, they are highly treasured by the receiver. I didn't fully understand at the time, but there was a reason for me receiving the coin far beyond me doing something deserving. In retrospect, it was all a part of the process to get me to my purpose. I had assumed that once I was done with

AIT, it was over. In 2003, I didn't know much about mainstream and commercialized cooking ventures. My focus then was to earn a living to take care of my children and that didn't include being a chef. I didn't seize the opportunity that was available in the military culinary industry, mainly because of my lack of knowledge and direction during that time of my life. I'm fortunate to have another opportunity to seize every undertaking that is now available and open for me. My desire is to still continue to learn as much as I can about the culinary industry.

If you are an aspiring chef in the valley of decision about your purpose, seek a Higher Power. Your purpose comes from someone higher than yourself. Your Creator designed you to be bent a certain way. If what you are doing is not giving you satisfaction, then you will not be able to bring satisfaction to others. You can't give what you don't have. We all have many interests and we enjoy doing many things, but it's that thing that you would do even if you didn't get paid that will give you the most reward. We are designed to give of ourselves, to help others, and to function proficiently in our purpose. Someone is waiting for what you have to offer. Someone is looking for someone with your specific gifts. Being a chef gives you an opportunity to leave an unforgettable, yet imaginable impressions with people through our creative artistic culinary skills.

Passion is an ambition that has materialized into action. When you do something, do it with all your might, and be sure that your heart is in it. When your heart is in a particular thing, don't lose hope easily, and it will be something you always return to. For me, I kept returning to the profession of cooking throughout my journey, because it was the right pathway for me.

Valentine's Day Dinner

~~~~~

Parmesan Risotto
Lemon Butter Buerre Blanc Asparagus
Seared Scallops
Chocolate Mouse

PARMESAN RISOTTO

Ingredients (7 servings)

10 to 12 cups chicken broth
2 tablespoons olive oil
2 tablespoons plus 1 tsp. butter, divided
1 medium onion, chopped
2 1/2 cups risotto rice
3/4 cup dry white wine
1/2 teaspoon salt
1/2 cup freshly grated parmesan cheese, plus more for serving
1/2 teaspoon freshly ground black pepper
1/4 cup flat-leaf parsley, chopped

Directions

1. Bring chicken broth to a simmer in a medium pot. Keep at a simmer, covered, over low heat.

2. Heat the olive oil and 2 tbsp butter over medium heat in a heavy-bottomed 8-qt. pot. Add onion and sauté, stirring occasionally, until onions are translucent and beginning to turn golden, for about 10 minutes.

3. Add rice and sauté, stirring constantly, until just the edges of the grains look translucent (about 3 minutes).

4. Add dry white wine and 1/2 teaspoon salt and cook, stirring, until wine is completely absorbed by rice. Add about 1/2 cup hot broth to rice and cook, stirring constantly, until broth is completely absorbed by rice; reduce heat to medium-low if mixture starts to boil. Continue adding broth 1/2 cup at a

time, stirring until each addition is absorbed before adding the next, until rice is just tender to the bite (15 to 30 minutes; you will have broth left over). Keep rice at a constant simmer.

5. Remove rice from heat and stir in parmesan, pepper, parsley, remaining 1 tsp. butter, and salt to taste. For a looser risotto, stir in 1 to 2 cups remaining broth. Serve immediately.

6. Sprinkle more parmesan on top.

LEMON BUERRE BLANC ASPARAGUS

Ingredients (4 servings)

2 tablespoons fresh lemon juice
4 tablespoons dry white wine
2 shallots, finely chopped
1 tablespoon crème fraiche
Salt and pepper
1 cup cold butter, cut into 16 cubes
1 bunch asparagus (about 1 pound), cleaned and trimmed
1 tablespoon olive oil
Kosher salt and freshly ground black pepper

Directions

1. Preheat the oven to 375 degrees F.

2. Toss the asparagus with the olive oil on a rimmed baking sheet and season with salt and pepper. Roast until slightly tender to the bite (about 10 minutes).

3. In a medium saucepan over medium-high heat, bring the lemon juice, wine, and shallots to a boil. Continue boiling the mixture for 3 to 5 minutes, until it reduces and thickens slightly. Add the crème fraiche to the glaze and boil it for an additional 2 minutes.

4. Add the butter, one cube at a time, whisk each piece of butter and allow it to fully dissolve before adding the next one. When the last of butter has just melted, remove the pan from the heat and strain out the shallots, if desired.

5. Season the Buerre Blanc sauce with salt and pepper and serve immediately.

SEARED SCALLOPS

Ingredients 4 servings

1-1/4 pounds dry sea scallops
Salt
Freshly ground black pepper
3 tablespoons butter, divided
1 tablespoon olive oil
2 tablespoons dry white wine
2 tablespoons freshly squeezed lemon juice
Zest of 1 lemon
2 tablespoons cream

Directions

1. Season the scallops on both sides with salt and fresh ground pepper and set aside.

2. Using a hot heavy skillet, add the olive oil and 1 tablespoon

of the butter. As soon as it is hot, add the scallops in a single layer.

3. Cook for 1 to 1-1/2 minutes per side (depending on the size), transferring them, one by one, to a plate as soon as they are cooked through. Cover loosely with foil to keep warm.

4. Add another tablespoon of butter to the pan, heat until frothy. Then deglaze the pan with dry white wine. Stir in the lemon juice, zest and any juices that have accumulated on the plate with the scallops.

5. Combine well, stir in the cream and the last tablespoon of butter. Remove from the heat as soon as the butter is melted.

6. Drizzle sauce on scallops.

CHOCOLATE MOUSSE

Ingredients (6 servings)

4 egg yolks
1/4 cup sugar
1 cup whipping (heavy) cream
1 package (6 ounces) semisweet chocolate chips (1 cup)
1 1/2 cups whipping (heavy) cream
1 teaspoon Amaretto Liqueur or syrup

Directions

1. Beat egg yolks in small bowl with electric mixer on high speed for about 3 minutes until lemon colored. Gradually beat in sugar.

2. Heat 1 cup whipping cream in 2-quart saucepan over medium heat until hot. Gradually stir at least half of the hot whipping cream into egg yolk mixture (Tempering); stir back into hot cream in saucepan.

3. Add Amaretto. Cook over low heat for about 5 minutes, stirring constantly, until mixture thickens (do not boil).

4. Stir in chocolate chips until melted. Cover and refrigerate for about 2 hours, stirring occasionally, just until chilled.

5. Beat 1 1/2 cups whipping cream in chilled medium bowl with electric mixer on high speed until stiff. Fold chocolate mixture into whipped cream. Spoon mixture into serving bowls. Immediately refrigerate any remaining dessert after serving.

CHAPTER 6
Embracing My Call to Cook

"I've come to believe that each of us has a personal calling that's as unique as a fingerprint—and that the best way to succeed is to discover what you love and then find a way to offer it to others in the form of a service, working hard, and allowing the energy of the universe to lead you."

Oprah Winfrey

Embracing your call means to give import to your life and fulfillment for walking in your purpose. There are some rocky moments that I've faced, but, with God, all things are possible. My journey was not easy by far, but I'm accomplishing everything I wanted to and am actively pursuing my goals. With God's grace, the work that has been started will be completed.

It took me the last five years to finally realize, I'm at my best-being self-employed and attending to my first ministry, which is family. I have been released from outside perceptions and stereotypes and I'm content. I'm not searching for that "right" thing or doing what I think other people think I should be doing. I'm no longer conforming to what the world thinks I should be or should have accomplished by now. I'm me, uniquely and wonderfully made.

Today, I am embracing my calling and am having fun teaching and learning about cooking. I'm enjoying catering. I love helping and encouraging others, alongside spending time with my family. At certain times, I felt I wasn't good enough, as though I should have been in another place in my life. I had envisioned myself already being a published author, already completing my degree, or already having an established career. It took me going through difficult challenges to overcome comparisons and world ideologies, but I realized that there are other plans for me—I only need to embrace my calling. These plans are to prosper me and not harm me. Embracing the call, I pursued my dreams and am now accomplishing my goals. My passion has driven me to my purpose.

Some of the benefits I have experienced as entrepreneur versus being employed are freedom, versatility, spontaneity, creativity and more flexibility with my time. Yes, there are careers that offer these benefits, but you may not find them all in one as I have in my chosen entrepreneurship. In my catering business, I have the freedom of setting my schedule, and I can be spontaneous in my life and with my family. I'm afforded opportunities to work with people and help them create memorable experiences, while I learn from them as well. Although I may become busy with working in my business, I'm also allowed to plan my downtime on my own terms.

But being in business alone can sometimes be overwhelming and stressful. Not only am I investing in myself, but am also investing in others. I'm fortunate for my husband and other resources that help my business, but as an entrepreneur, I'm ultimately responsible for my earnings. This responsibility has made me innovative. My only limitations are the ones I set for myself. A grilled cheese sandwich is ordinarily just cheese and bread until it's made differently, extraordinary. Considering how competitive the catering industry is, every dish has to be unique and original.

Entrepreneurship has also been supportive of my personal responsibilities as a wife and mom. My husband has a challenging, but rewarding career, so, most of the time, I am solely responsible for taking care of my home and the needs of my children. We truly help each other and are blessed to have quality time as a family. However, I quickly realized how much I'm needed at home with a big family and younger children, while also actively fulfilling my purpose. When the choice between family and a fulltime career away from home became obvious, I chose self-employment. I was afraid that I didn't know how to be an entrepreneur, and, in truth, sometimes I'm still afraid. But I realized that I have to do it afraid or else it's not going to get done. Sometimes society will label a person and deem them unfit, because they don't work a nine-to-five; however, I came to the understanding that I have to know my own personal worth and that it's not just about me when there is family involved. My desires are to be an example for my children and siblings, and also to always please Him who has given my calling to me.

~~~~~

When I'm in the zone working, catering, and doing things that chefs do, I hardly notice the time passing by. I feel liberated, I feel encouraged, I feel inspired, and I feel fulfilled. It can sometimes act as therapy for me. Nothing else really matters to me while I'm cooking, except doing quality work and meeting the needs of my clients. As a caterer, my clients are not only the person who hired me to work for them, but also the friends and family they invite to enjoy my services. It's a big task, but I know I have what it takes.

As a result of making this decision to become an entrepreneur, my family and I can continue to receive the blessings of my calling and purpose. Being blessed is not always about monetary or material gifts; we are blessed spiritually and we can pass on a legacy for generations. My children may not want to become chefs, but I can inspire them to go after their own passion and find purpose in their passion. My youngest daughter, Brook-Lynne, likes to bake. She's not old enough to read directions, but she still gets the urge to mix ingredients and crack eggs when we make cakes, brownies, and cookies together. I personally prefer cooking over baking, so it's good that she loves the latter.

My oldest son, EJ, likes to watch Food Network and the Cooking Channel. He is also an avid athlete and enjoys fishing. These extracurricular activities are priceless teaching opportunities for my children. I'm grateful my mama and grandmother shared the kitchen with me. In my own childhood, gardening was my favorite activity and while my least favorite (of course) was chores. Nevertheless, I learned. I got an experience that is treasured and can be passed on to my family. I taught my own children how to plant and harvest vegetables, although we've had more attempts at planting than successful harvesting. Still, every year, we start over and try again.

Being an entrepreneur, I can use my time wisely and cherish the time with my family, sharing in their interest and encouraging them to follow their passion. I hope my journey inspires someone else to find their purpose and exercise the necessary faith to accomplish their dreams.

Too Close for Comfort Foods

~~~~~

Venison Chili Beans
Soulful of Cheese and Macaroni
Not Your Mama's Meatloaf
White Chocolate Bread Pudding w/ Bourbon Sauce

VENISON CHILI BEANS

Ingredients (6-8 Servings)

1-pound lean ground beef
1-pound ground venison
1 teaspoon salt
1 teaspoon black pepper
1 teaspoon garlic powder
1 teaspoon paprika
2 tablespoons chili powder
1 teaspoon ground cumin
3 (15 ounce) cans dark red kidney beans
3 (15 ounce) cans pinto beans
3 (14.5 ounce) stewed tomatoes
1 large red tomato, blanched & diced
2 stalks celery, chopped
1 red bell pepper, chopped
1 onion, chopped

1 teaspoon parsley
1 teaspoon basil
1 ounce Worcestershire sauce
1/2 cup red wine

Directions

1. In a large skillet over medium-high heat, cook ground beef and venison until evenly browned. Drain off grease, and season to taste with salt and pepper.

2. In a Dutch oven, combine the cooked beef, kidney beans, pinto beans, tomatoes, celery, and red bell pepper. Season with garlic powder, paprika, chili powder, cumin, parsley, basil and Worcestershire sauce. Stir to distribute ingredients evenly.

3. Cook on high for 6 hours. Pour in the wine during the last 2 hours.

SOULFUL OF CHEESE AND MACARONI

Ingredients (6 servings)

1 pound uncooked elbow pasta
2 tablespoons butter
1/4 cup all-purpose flour
3 cups fat-free milk
1 (12-oz.) can fat-free evaporated milk
1 cup (4 oz.) shredded smoked Gouda cheese
1/2 cup (2 oz.) shredded 1.5% reduced-fat sharp Cheddar cheese
3 ounces fat-free cream cheese, softened
1/2 teaspoon salt
1/4 teaspoon ground mustard
1/4 teaspoon ground white pepper, divided
Vegetable cooking spray
1 tablespoon butter, melted

Directions

1. Preheat oven to 350°. Prepare elbow macaroni pasta according to package directions. Drain macaroni.

2. Melt 2 tablespoons butter in a Dutch oven over medium heat. Gradually whisk in flour, whisking constantly for 1 minute.

3. Gradually whisk in milk and evaporated milk until smooth. Cook, whisking constantly, for 8 to 10 minutes or until slightly thickened. Whisk in Gouda cheese, cheddar cheese, and cream cheese. Stir in ground white pepper and ground mustard until smooth.

4. Remove from heat, and stir in pasta.

5. Pour pasta mixture into a 13- x 9-inch baking dish coated with cooking spray.

6. Bake at 350° for 30 minutes or until golden and bubbly. Let stand for 5 minutes before serving.

NOT YOUR MAMA'S MEATLOAF

Ingredients (4-6 Servings)

1 tablespoon onion, minced
1 tablespoon bell pepper, minced
2 pounds lean Ground Beef
1 large Egg
1/2 Cup Bread Crumbs
1 teaspoon salt
1 teaspoon black pepper
1 teaspoon paprika
1 teaspoon oregano
1 teaspoon parsley
1 teaspoon basil
2 Tablespoon Worcestershire sauce
1 cup jalapeño peppers, sliced
1 cup shredded Mozzarella Cheese

Sauce

1 cup ketchup
1/4 cup brown sugar, tightly packed
1 Tablespoon red wine vinegar
2 cloves garlic, crushed
1 Tablespoon Worcestershire sauce

Directions

1. Preheat a convection oven to 320° Fahrenheit
2. Line a 9x5 inch loaf pan first with parchment paper.

3. In a large mixing bowl, combine ground beef, bread crumbs, basil, oregano, parsley, paprika, salt, pepper, onion, and bell pepper, jalapeño peppers, egg, and Worcestershire sauce. Knead all ingredients until combined.

4. Shape a long log with 2/3 of the meat mixture and fit it inside the loaf pan. Make a groove in the middle and add the mozzarella cheese to it. Shape remaining meat as the top half of the loaf, sealing the edges.

5. In a small mixing bowl whisk together ketchup, brown sugar, Worcestershire sauce, red wine vinegar, garlic, salt, and cayenne pepper. Pour half of this mixture over the meatloaf, reserving the remaining half for later.

6. Bake in the middle of the preheated oven for 40 minutes.

7. Spread with the remaining sauce, Increase temperature to 400 degrees and bake for another 20 minutes.

8. Let rest for 10 minutes before serving.

WHITE CHOCOLATE BREAD PUDDING

Ingredients (8 servings)

2 (12-oz.) cans evaporated milk

6 large eggs, lightly beaten

1 (16-oz.) day-old French bread loaf, cubed

2 cups white chocolate chips

1 1/2 cups sugar

5 tablespoons vanilla extract

1/4 cup butter, cut into 1/2-inch cubes and softened

Directions

1. Preheat oven to 350°. Whisk together evaporated milk, eggs, and 1 cup water in a large bowl until well blended. Stir in sugar and vanilla extract and white chocolate chips. Stir in butter, blending well.

2. Layer bread cubes in a greased 13x 9 inch baking dish.

3. Pour pudding mixture over bread cubes in greased 13 x 9inch baking dish.

4. Bake at 350° for 35 to 45 minutes or until set and crust is golden. Remove from oven, and let stand for 2 minutes. Serve with bourbon sauce (optional).

CHAPTER 7

Defining My Purpose as a Chef

"You can make many plans, but the Lord's purpose will prevail."

Proverbs 19:21

Culinary arts is defined as the preparation of food using heat and cooking techniques, the word "culinary" coming from the Latin word "about the kitchen." Cooking is a great art and food its creation. Culinary also includes different types of cuisines: Chinese, American, French, Italian, and much more. Cuisines are a different way of cooking foods according to individual cultures or traditions. American cuisine is unique in that there is mix of cultures—it's like a melting pot. The cook or the chef creates something unique and can fuses two cuisines together to wield the art of cooking.

Becoming a chef is a calling because it is a service. A calling is ministering to others' needs, just like teaching, nursing, and being in law enforcement are all different vocations or careers. As a chef, you are using your gifts and talents not only for the benefit of nourishment or yourself, but also for the nourishment of others, so I don't take being a chef and a caterer lightly. I know my services are worthy. After each level of success that is obtained, there will be another challenge to strengthen you for your blessing.

The calling placed on your life is too important to ignore. It is essential and beneficial to you and everyone connected to you. There is a bigger picture other than working to receive a paycheck or to take care of your daily living expenses. Each and every one of us is born with a gift, whether you believe it or not. When you seek, know, and activate your gift, then you are walking in your purpose. If everyone walked in their purpose, there would be so many needs being met without anxiety or worry.

I once had anxiety about what I should do with my life. Once I came to realize my calling and decided to walk in my purpose, I knew exactly what I should be doing. That worry is for no use. I may not have all that I want yet but I have all that I need. I understand and believe that, if I keep walking in my purpose and fulfilling my calling as a chef, I can have the desires of my heart. It's not selfish; rather, it's selfless to walk in your purpose, because you are helping others. I sometimes wonder about the potential of a homeless person. I know life happens and, at any given time, it could be me, but I'm thankful for the grace that I received to finally get it right and not run from my purpose. We all are called to do something. Find it and walk in it.

~~~~~

I once was persuaded by society to believe that the cooking profession was unworthy of pursuit and trivial. I wanted to be a cook or chef when I grew up, but I thought this was not good enough. If you visit a hospital cafeteria or fine dining restaurant, nothing is screaming glamorous about a person wearing a chef coat, apron and head wear. There's no nail polish, no makeup, no earrings. None of that matters to me now, because my mindset is different. I couldn't fathom the endless possibilities and opportunities in the culinary arts industry, until recently when I actually explored them.

The perception that is most important to me is that my food looks and tastes good and my clients receive excellent service. Today, you turn on the Food Network TV channel and you see glamour. You see more than the magnificent culinary creations—you also see the smiles and see the women chefs wearing makeup and being gorgeous. I once wished to become one of the Food Network or Cooking Channel stars, but when the direction of my life changed, that big idea also changed: I did an evaluation and focused on my purpose as a chef and becoming a caterer. I still can become famous like those television stars, just not in the same ways. It's important to pay attention, not so much to your personal and immediate desires, but to the whole of your true purpose.

We must respect the pathway God has chosen for our lives, regardless of public opinion, because we are servants with a bigger purpose. It's hard sometimes not to get distracted but we often do. There are times, you may want to give up because it doesn't feel right or it doesn't turn out how we thought it should. I didn't give up on my passion—I just knew there was a different pathway, a better opportunity to prepare myself for in order to receive the full blessing from waiting on the appropriate time and season, and doing what is best.

There is still work to be done in my personal and professional life. Writing this book has given me a chance to reflect on how fulfilling my purpose strengthened my faith. I know I can't do any of this in my own strength. I recognize the need to trust in God and not lean only on my own understanding of things. Every path I followed was to lead me to a closer relationship with my God and helped me to be patient and obedient. My quality of life has changed, because I'm not worried about being better than someone else. I'm not in competition with anyone, because I'm not made to be like anyone else. I only want to be a better person than I was yesterday.

My cooking is also not supposed to look exactly like another chef's. My food is not supposed to taste like someone else's, no matter how closely related the recipes. My skill set is different. We all put our own unique touch into our recipes and we are all unique in our own right. You ever heard someone say that someone's cooking was so good that they put their foot in it? It's an idiom meaning you cooked the dish so wonderfully that someone wants to plunge themselves into it. Even though they ate the same dish before, yours is better. Yes, we are taught and trained to uphold a certain standard, but ultimately we are going to do things differently. *Throwdown with Bobby Flay* on Food Network is a prime example of someone who works with personal flair. Bobby Flay is a celebrity chef and restaurateur. The show is interesting, because although the competitors are making similar dishes in a food competition, the food all looks and tastes different, because of the different people who each putting their own unique flavor and flair to it. They both present appealing and quality dishes—it all just comes down to a particular taste over another. This lesson from the kitchen taught me that fulfilling my purpose has shown me how uniquely and wonderfully made I really am.

STEPS TO FULFILLING YOUR PURPOSE

Step 1:

Once you have determined your purpose as a chef, do an evaluation of where you are in regards to your skills and talents. Determine what it will take to reach your desired goal (certification, degree, mentorship, culinary institute, etc.). Do a personal SWOT (Strengths, Weaknesses, Opportunities, and Threats) analysis.

Step 2

Make this a matter of prayer and seek the advice of the Master Creator on how to proceed. After all, He designed you for a specific purpose, and He knows best how to fulfill it. Also, seek the advice of people in your field that have accomplished what you are aspiring to accomplish. Do this continuously at each level in the process.

Step 3

Develop a vision board (pictorial) and write down your vision. This will remind you of your goals and objectives, keep you focused, and give you comfort when you reach difficult places. It will also let you know when to celebrate each complete milestone.

Step 4

Remember to eat the elephant one bite at a time. When creating a recipe for a culinary masterpiece, you must develop a step-by-step procedure to accomplish your goal. You must do the same when developing a strategy to fulfill your purpose. You should have short-term (immediate) and long-term goals and develop the steps to accomplish them.

Step 5

Once you are headed in the right direction, resources, opportunities, and the right people will show up. Be cognizant of your surroundings and expect them. Sometimes it will be like digging for gold, but keep digging—eventually you will get your reward. Other times, it will be like walking down the street and finding a hundred-dollar bill just lying there on the sidewalk. Your objective is to be intentional about your goal and tenacious in its pursuit. Being a chef is your calling. Walking in it will bring you much fulfillment.

Sunday Dinner

~~~~~

Linda's Eggplant Rice Dressing
Mama's Old Fashioned Potato Salad
Braised Short Ribs
Southern Okra Succotash

LINDA'S EGGPLANT RICE DRESSING

Ingredients (8 Servings)

1 Tablespoon oil

2 large eggplants, peeled and diced

1/2 cup of onion, chopped

1/2 cup bell pepper, chopped

2 cups celery, chopped

1 cup gizzards, cut

1 pound ground beef

16 oz. Savoie's Dressing Mix

1 teaspoon garlic powder

1 teaspoon black pepper

1 teaspoon salt

1 bay leaf

3 cups cooked rice

Directions

1. In a stock pot bring gizzards to a boil until tender.

2. Heat oil in pan and add eggplant, onion, bell pepper, celery, and stir. Cook for about 30 minutes. Set aside.

3. Remove gizzards and chop.

4. In a larger pot season and cook ground beef and stir in Savoie's dressing mix.

5. Add eggplant, onion, bell pepper, celery, and gizzards to ground meat mixture. Cook for 30 minutes.

6. Add rice, bay leaf, salt and pepper. Fluff with fork.

MAMA'S OLD FASHIONED POTATO SALAD

Ingredients (8–10 servings)

6 eggs
12 russet potatoes, peeled
3 teaspoons salt
3 teaspoons paprika
3 teaspoons garlic powder
2 tablespoons mustard
3 tablespoons sweet dill relish
5 tablespoons mayonnaise
Freshly ground black pepper
Fresh parsley, minced for garnish

Directions

1. In a large pot, hard-boil the eggs. Drain and shock eggs. Peel and then dice eggs. Set aside.

2. In a large pot, boil whole potatoes until fully cooked. Drain water. Let potatoes cool for about 5 minutes. In a large bowl mash potatoes using potato masher. **Note:** potatoes and eggs can boil simultaneously.

3. Add all remaining ingredients, including the eggs and mix.

4. Garnish with parsley. Serve immediately, or refrigerate until serving time.

BRAISED SHORT RIBS

Ingredients (8-10 servings)

2 Tablespoons Canola oil

3 pounds Short ribs, cut into individual ribs

2 Tablespoon Creole seasoning

1 cup onions, diced

1/2 cup celery, chopped

1 cup carrot, sliced

1 cup chopped fresh or canned tomatoes

2 Tablespoons garlic, minced

1/2 cup Red wine vinegar

2 Tablespoon Worcestershire sauce

3 Bay leaves

2 teaspoons Black pepper

2-quart Beef broth

1/4 cup green scallion, chopped

Directions

1. Heat oil in a Dutch oven or large, heavy covered pot over high heat.

2. Season ribs with Creole seasoning. When pot is heated add ribs without crowding them and sear on all sides until they form a brown crust.

3. When all ribs have browned, add onions, celery and carrot. Sauté for 1 minute to brown lightly.

4. Stir in tomatoes, garlic, vinegar, Worcestershire sauce, bay leaves, pepper and enough broth to just cover ribs. Bring to a boil, reduce heat to gently simmering, cover and simmer until very tender, for about 2 1/2 hours.

5. When plating, spoon sauce over ribs and garnish with chopped scallion.

SOUTHERN OKRA SUCCOTASH

Ingredients (8 servings)

3 medium ears corn or frozen corn
1 tablespoon canola oil
1/2 pound fresh or frozen baby butter (lima) beans
1/2 cup chopped andouille or smoked ham or pickled pork optional
1 cup sliced fresh or frozen okra, thawed
1 cup chopped Vidalia or other sweet onion
1/2 cup chopped sweet bell pepper (green, red, yellow, orange or combination)
1/2 tablespoon minced garlic
1 teaspoon kosher salt, or to taste
1/4 teaspoon freshly cracked black pepper, or to taste
1/4 teaspoon Creole or Cajun seasoning, or to taste, optional
1 cup halved grape tomatoes
2 teaspoons fresh parsley, chopped

Directions

1. Use a sharp serrated knife to carefully cut off the root end of the corn, remove husks and silks, and cut corn off of the cob. Use dull edge of the knife to scrape down the milk. Set aside.

2. Cook corn using your favorite method, or sauté frozen corn meanwhile, add pickled pork to a small saucepan and cover with water. Bring to a boil for 15minutes, until tender. Later, transfer to skillet with slotted spoon and reserve water.

3. Sauté garlic, onions, peppers, celery in oil in a large skillet, for about 3 minutes or until onions are clear.

4. Add the corn, okra, lima beans, tomatoes meat and seasonings to the skillet. Add some of the reserved cooking water, a little at a time, only if mixture is too dry. Reduce heat to medium low, cook and stir until everything is heated through, add parsley. Taste and adjust seasonings as needed. Serve immediately.

CHAPTER 8

What You Can Learn in the Kitchen

"As in cooking, and in life, you must always follow the directions."

Chef Diana

A chef's hat is something more than just something you put on. There's a lot of responsibility that comes with it: responsibility to stay true to your calling, responsibility to your peers to be a good example, responsibility to your customers to provide a good meal, and a responsibility to the civic authorities to keep a Grade A kitchen. You achieve most of this by following instructions. Below are answers to questions that I myself asked in the process of pursuing my passion. They will capsulize everything that you have read so far in the book.

How do you learn patience in the kitchen? What is the life principle associated with patience?

Patience is defined as the capacity to tolerate trouble or suffering without getting angry. If you are not willing to wait for something, you will never possess it. By having patience, you earn the very thing you are waiting for and you will come to appreciate the value of it more. Patience builds character.

How do you learn consistency in the kitchen? What is the life principle associated with consistency?

Consistency is uniformity. By being consistent in the kitchen, you embody excellence and are constantly building and improving upon what you learn. In culinary school, my instructors taught me that cooking is all about consistency, whether controlling fire (heat required for a particular recipe) or building flavor.

How do you learn determination in the kitchen? What is the life principle associated with determination?

You gain determination in the kitchen by showing up each day. Doing the work gives you the opportunity to see the fruits of your labor. You must finish the work you start and stay on course.

How do you learn resilience in the kitchen? What is the life principle associated with resistance?

Resilience is the capacity to recover quickly from difficulties. In professional kitchens or in your home kitchen, you must learn how to bounce back and accept things gracefully. Although you worked hard to prepare your family meal, they may dislike it. Don't get discouraged and, instead, learn from it. Failing once does not constitute failing always.

Resiliency is like removing the backbone of a chicken. Remove the backbone of a chicken then it becomes more flexible. Although the bone is no longer intact, it retains its integrity. In life, you sometimes lose—the recompense comes when you withstand the difficulty of the trials.

How do you learn endurance in the kitchen? What is the life principle associated with endurance?

Endurance develops your strength. Learning endurance is the true grit required to be an overcomer. Working in the professional kitchen, there is seldom time for breaks. The work is mostly non-stop. By enduring long hours in the professional kitchen, I developed my character and will. I learned that I was made of more than sugar, spice, and everything nice. I became as tough as the sugar cane stalk I used to chew as a child.

How do you learn to trust in the kitchen? What is the life principle associated with trust?

In the professional kitchen, every person is important. You expect the dishwasher to do their job, just as you expect the sous chef and prep cook to do theirs. We develop working relationships and it helps us to depend on each other. Sometimes, you may be let down, but you've got to keep moving forward to complete the task. I learned to trust my instincts and judgments. Trusting people is a two-way street.

Another valuable lesson that I learned in the kitchen is to place my trust in objects more than in people. I rely more on my kitchen utensils and equipment. I can't bake bread without the heat of an oven.

How do you learn discipline in the kitchen? What is the life principle associated with discipline?

A disciplined chef does not compromise their integrity. There is a certain expectation when serving others. In the kitchen, discipline is learned through practice. The floor should be so clean that you could eat off of it. But you won't, because there is a rule or code of behavior that should also be followed.

How do you learn strength in the kitchen? What is the life principle associated with strength?

Lessons drawn from the kitchen granted me the inner strength to stay focused on my purpose. It gave me the inner strength to achieve goals and to persevere through hardships and negativity. The kitchen is structured to make a cook stronger, both physically through labor and mentally through demanding quick thinking and efficiency.

What are your closing thoughts on life lessons learned in the kitchen?

Once the carrots are sliced, the onions are chopped, and the rice is cooked, there is no turning back. You can't rearrange them or revert it back to its previous state. In the kitchen, I learned many lessons that are applicable to life. But one thing that is for certain is that change is constant and also inevitable. I always take things with a grain of salt and learn to embrace challenges. Lessons I learned from the kitchen not only made me stronger and wiser, but they have also helped me to know my worth and that I'm built for whatever life throws at me.

I understand that my Creator would never put more on me than I can handle, and that's why he gave me these gifts to use. No matter what I plan, ultimately His way will supersede. It's like planning a menu and making sure you gather all the ingredients, but no amount of preparation can give you the wisdom you need to improvise during unforeseen circumstances. In the kitchen, I learned to be an innovator. In a world full of culinary artists, cooks, and chefs, you have to find your place and set yourself apart. A few times, I have had to change a menu or change an event arrangement on short notice to appease my clients. Always have a backup plan even when you don't have a backup plan.

Another lesson is that things don't always go as planned or the way you think they should in life. Some things can be fixed and some things stay broken. You can hide small imperfections in a cake by putting the icing on it, but you can't hide what's on the inside once you slice it. I learned to be intentional about what I want and to follow through. The most important part of the recipe is the directions—in life, you also need directions, and once received, they must be followed.

Some things you just have to wait for. John C. Maxwell says it best: "God prepares leaders in a slow cooker, not in a microwave oven. More important than the ultimate goal is the work God does in us while we wait. Waiting deepens and matures us, levels our perspective, and broadens our understanding." Tests of time determine whether we can endure seasons of seemingly unfruitful preparations and indicate whether we can recognize and seize the opportunities that come our way as a result. In cooking individual dishes like osso bucco, you can't rush. It's going to take some time: it passes by so fast when you're having fun or doing something you love, but when you're bored, it seemingly moves slow. Just like osso bucco, you are His culinary masterpiece slowly simmering and intertwining all the ingredients, including "thyme," to create beautiful richness to be savored at the end of its cooking duration.

Earlier, I expressed how being a cook or chef isn't too glamorous. You are sweating your heart and soul out behind a stove in a hot kitchen. You literally sometimes look a hot mess. But remember that most people only see what you appear to be and looks can be deceiving—only a few people truly experience what you really are. When people eat, they eat with their eyes first; if it is not appealing, they probably won't eat it at all or even attempt to taste it, so make it look good.

Finally, you must learn to gain perspective and truly appreciate the little things in life. It may not seem as if I have it all but, in reality, I have just what I need and what is willed to me. Make the most of it and enjoy it. Lessons are learned by the choices made. I choose to accept my calling. I choose to do great things. I choose to learn from my mistakes. I choose to invest in myself and in my family. I choose to learn. I chose to become a better person. I choose to be a chef and you can too!

Cooking Takes Thyme

~~~~~

Garlic Braised Osso Bucco
Roast Thyme Chicken
Thyme Butter Sauce

GARLIC BRAISED OSSO BUCCO

Ingredients (4 servings)

4 thick beef shanks (3-4 pounds)

1 teaspoon Salt

Peppercorns, crushed

1 teaspoon Garlic powder

3 tablespoons vegetable oil (1 1/2 tablespoons for the shanks + 1 1/2 tablespoons for the vegetables)

1 medium yellow onion, chopped

1 medium carrot, chopped

1 stalk celery, chopped

2 clove garlic, minced

1 tablespoon tomato paste

2 cups tomato purée

2 cups dry white wine

2 tablespoons chopped fresh thyme

Directions

1. Preheat the oven to 300F and put the rack in the middle position. Season the shanks generously with salt, garlic powder and peppercorns. Prep the remaining ingredients.

2. Heat the oil in a Dutch oven over medium-high heat. When the oil is hot and shimmering, add the shanks to the pan with space between them. Sear the shanks, pressing the meat to the pan occasionally, until they are very brown (about 2-4 minutes). Turn and brown the second side. Remove the shanks to a plate.

3. Turn the heat down to medium and add the carrot, onion and celery. Sprinkle the vegetables lightly with salt and pepper. Cook, stirring occasionally, for 3 minutes, then stir in the garlic. Stirring constantly, until the vegetables are soft.

4. Add the tomato paste and stir to caramelize it well for 2-3 minutes. Add the tomato purée and white wine to the Dutch oven. Stir and scrape to release the brown bits from the bottom of the pan. Place the browned shanks into the liquid, and pour in any juices it stored while it rested.

5. Add enough water to come up almost cover the shanks. Cover and roast in the oven, turning 3-4 times until the meat almost falls off the bone (about 2-2 1/2 hours). Stir in the thyme 15 minutes before taking the shanks out of the oven.

ROAST THYME CHICKEN

Ingredients (6-8 servings)

2 (2.5 pound) whole chickens
Salt
Pepper
2 large onions, quartered
6 shallots, finely chopped
8 cloves garlic, peeled
3 tablespoons olive oil
1/2 cup butter, softened
8 sprigs thyme, fresh

Directions

1. Preheat oven to 375 degrees F (190 degrees C). Lightly grease a medium baking dish.

2. Arrange chickens in the center of the prepared baking ban. Spread butter over the chickens, and season with salt and pepper. Drizzle onions, shallots and garlic with olive oil. Place onions, shallots, and garlic in and around chicken. Line each chicken with thyme sprigs.

3. Bake for 20 minutes in the preheated oven then increase temperature to 400 degrees F and continue baking 30 minutes until an internal temperature of 165 degrees F and juices run clear. Allow to rest before serving. Garnish with lemon.

THYME BUTTER SAUCE

Ingredients

2 shallots, minced
6 sprigs fresh thyme
Salt and pepper
2 cups white wine
1/2 cup unsalted butter plus 2 Tbsp., divided
3 Tbsp. fresh thyme, chopped

Directions

1. In a medium saucepan over medium heat, add the shallots, sprigs of thyme, and wine. Cook the sauce until reduced by three fourths.

2. Lower the heat and add the butter, whisking until melted.

3. Add salt and pepper and the chopped fresh thyme. Remove from heat.

4. Note: This sauce can be spooned over salmon, pork, or chicken.

About the Author

Diana Riley is an executive chef, entrepreneur, veteran, mother, wife, and woman of faith. Before pursuing her career as a chef, she served nine years with the Louisiana Army National Guard, for which she received an Army Achievement Medal and Iraq Campaign Medal. She received a degree in culinary arts in 2010 from Nicholls State University's Chef John Folse Culinary Institute, where she was taught by prestigious chefs such as John Folse. She also received her certificate in entrepreneurship training from the Whitman School of Management VWISE in 2011. She is currently earning her degree in culinary business administration, once again at the Chef John Folse Culinary Institute. Riley is also a member of the Baton Rouge Chapter American Culinary Federation.

Riley currently resides in Plaquemine, Louisiana with her husband, Barry Riley Sr, and their six children. She is the owner and executive chef at The Kitchen Table Catering Company, LLC. When she is not busy cooking delicious meals for her clients and loved ones, she volunteers her time at her church as a youth mentor.

WE WANT TO HEAR FROM YOU!!!

If this book has made a difference in your life Diana would be delighted to hear about it.

Leave a review on Amazon.com!

BOOK DIANA TO SPEAK AT YOUR NEXT EVENT!

Send an email to: booking@publishyourgift.com

LEARN MORE ABOUT DIANA AT:

www.DianaKitchenTable.com

FOLLOW DIANA ON SOCIAL MEDIA:

  @diana_mamachef

"EMPOWERING YOU TO IMPACT GENERATIONS"

WWW.PUBLISHYOURGIFT.COM

www.ingramcontent.com/pod-product-compliance
Lightning Source LLC
Chambersburg PA
CBHW041958080526
44588CB00021B/2788